KT-167-602

50 Queers Who Changed the World

A CELEBRATION OF LGBTQ+ ICONS

DAN JONES

Illustrated by Michele Rosenthal

hardie grant books

Contents

Introduction 6

Freddie Mercury 8
Alison Bechdel 10
Christopher Isherwood 12
Radclyffe Hall 14
Gladys Bentley 16

kd lang 18
Camille Paglia 20
Keith Haring 22
Barbara Gittings 24

RuPaul 26
Chavela Vargas 28
Rock Hudson 30
James Baldwin 32
Lili Elbe 34
Quentin Crisp 36
Gertrude Stein 38
Harvey Milk 40

Patricia Highsmith 42
Peter Tatchell 44
Sylvia Rivera 46
Justin Vivian Bond 48
Virginia Woolf 50
George Takei 52

Jake Miller 54
Sally Ride 56
Andy Warhol 58

Billie Holiday *60*
Dan Savage *62*
Audre Lorde *64*
Sandra Bernhard *66*
Essex Hemphill *68*

Ellen DeGeneres *94*
Marlene Dietrich *96*
Armistead Maupin *98*

Candy Darling *70*
Oscar Wilde *72*
Lily Tomlin *74*
Alan Turing *76*
Michael Dillon *78*
Madonna *80*
Rachel Maddow *82*
Larry Kramer *84*
Laverne Cox *86*

Eleanor Roosevelt *100*
Leigh Bowery *102*
Ron Woodroof *104*
Frida Kahlo *106*

More Queer Heroes Who
Changed the World *108*
About the Author *111*
Acknowledgements *111*

Divine *88*
Stephen Tennant *90*
Allen Ginsberg *92*

Introduction

Meet 50 queer heroes of music, art, theatre and literature, tough-ass political activists and sugary pop culture icons, plus non-binary pioneers and gender non-conformists, gay codebreakers, trans revolutionaries, and lesbians in space. Some are meek and mild, others angry and volatile; some have been all but ignored by history, misunderstood or taken too soon, and others have burned brightly, loud-mouthed and wonderfully precocious. There are those born into privilege who risk it all by coming out, and those that have clawed their way out of the mire with talent and tenacity.

What makes a queer hero? You don't have to be gay, lesbian, bisexual, trans or unicorn (although it helps). What's needed is a queer-minded attitude, being an advocate and ally to civil equality, human rights, living life to the fullest, and leaving a queer legacy so others in the future can climb ever higher.

Across the decades, there are reoccurring themes and shared qualities. These queer heroes are motivated by love, sex, truth, and freedom, from the campaigning of Harvey Milk and the Aids awareness work of Larry Kramer to the warrior poetry of Audre Lorde and the intergalactic travels of Sally Ride. What sets them apart is a steadfastness, a bravery to live life against the rules, to ignore social convention and risk everything, from reputations to lives, to change the world.

Freddie Mercury

Wearer of sequined chest-baring one-pieces, eye-wateringly tight tights and bulging wet-look leather, toothy Freddie Mercury (born Farrokh Bulsara; 1946–91) was the impossibly camp frontman of legendary pop-rock outfit Queen. As a performer, Mercury would truss himself up in fetish gear with aviators, white vests, denim and studded bicep bands: outfits that seemed to scream GAY SEX! to his adoring – and surprisingly mainstream – fans, who would do little more than titter and tut at his balls-out sexuality.

In his early twenties, Mercury performed with a couple of forget-table bands and hawked vintage fashion at London's Kensington Market, finally joining fellow musicians Brian May and Roger Taylor to form Queen in 1970. He penned and performed 'Killer Queen' (1974), 'Bohemian Rhapsody' (1975), and 'Don't Stop Me Now' (1979), balancing a shy offstage persona with an eye-popping on-stage creation – his set with Queen at Live Aid in 1985 is thought of as the landmark rock performance.

The tabloid press loved reporting on Mercury's louche lifestyle. His antics filled column inches and grew his celebrity, but it proved a fickle relationship. By 1990, rumours of Mercury's HIV status saw him doorstepped at home and ambushed at airports; hacks who once celebrated Mercury's excess now slut-shamed him, and pictures of him looking thin and frail hit the front pages. He died the following year.

Although Mercury was criticised for not publicly engaging with lesbian and gay groups and HIV-awareness organisations (he did much to protect his privacy, and those around him), he dragged his own version of queerness – in all its scantily clad glory – into the mainstream.

 9

Alison Bechdel

Alison Bechdel (1960) is a 'Dyke to Watch Out For'. The impossibly geeky American cartoonist's long-running strip *Dykes to Watch Out For* (1983–2008) and celebrated memoirs *Fun Home* (2006) and *Are You My Mother?* (2012) mark her out as a unique queer artist and important cultural voice.

Bechdel drew comic-like art from a young age, found gender confounding and struggled to see a girl like herself reflected in contemporary culture. She realised she was gay as a student at Oberlin College, Ohio, in 1981, but this sudden awareness proved tricky. Around the same time, Bechdel discovered her father was bisexual – and deeply closeted – before he suddenly died. The autobiographical *Fun Home* deals with this unique situation: a coming-out story compounded by the tragedy of losing a parent who hid away their true desires. Moving to New York in 1981, Bechdel threw herself headfirst into the city's vibrant queer subculture of underground dance clubs and steamy lesbian meet-ups. She had to get it down on paper. Bechdel discovered a copy of *Gay Comix*, a compilation of comic art by gay men and lesbians, and felt inspired to do it herself.

For 25 years, *Dykes to Watch Out For* followed the highs and lows, ins and outs of American lesbian culture, and it was here she introduced the Bechdel Test, which a film or book can only pass if it features two women who have a conversation about something other than a man (now used widely to point out sexist media).

Today, Bechdel seems to be a little mystified, if not heart-warmed, by her success. In 1981, the job of nerdy comic artist hardly seemed to be a clever career choice, but over the years, Bechdel's work has met with huge acclaim. Her comic has a huge cult following and *Fun Home* was made into a hit Broadway musical. Bechdel has shown that, in popular culture, there is a place for the geeky lesbian in all her glory.

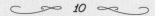

Christopher Isherwood

If there was ever a writer who could expertly conjure a deliciously pent-up, awkward sexuality, it is Christopher Isherwood (1904–86). The author of *Goodbye to Berlin* (1939) and *A Single Man* (1964) published his personal diaries late in life, which proved even more salacious and exciting than his fictional creations.

As a teen, Isherwood was more than a little precocious. He churned out stories and poems, created a literary fantasy world with his friend Edward Upward, and wrote plays with WH Auden. Asked to leave Cambridge University after deliberately ruining his exam paper, Isherwood spent a brief spell studying medicine before heading off where any self-respecting upper-middle class gay man would in 1929: to Weimar Berlin. By all accounts he threw himself crotch-first into the city's decadent, bohemian lifestyle and spent a lost, steamy summer exploring his sexuality. Years later, in *Christopher and His Kind* (1976), Isherwood revealed the story of his Berlin antics and relationship with Heinz Neddermeyer (before Heinz's arrest in 1937), securing his place as something of a con-temporary (and sexually accomplished) queer hero.

For a small man, Isherwood lived big: he travelled extensively and intrepidly, had sticky love affairs, became a practising Hindu, and wrote prolifically. *Goodbye to Berlin* was reworked by John Van Druten for the stage play *I Am a Camera* (1951), which was later adapted into the hugely successful musical *Cabaret* (1966). Isherwood's fame grew, but by 1953, he had other things on his mind and fell in love with handsome 18-year-old college student, Don Bachardy. After a tricky patch that inspired Isherwood's *A Single Man*, one of his finest works, the pair stayed together until Isherwood's death in 1986.

Radclyffe Hall

Many a geeky young lesbian has plumbed *The Well of Loneliness* (1928), Radclyffe Hall's taboo-breaking and gender-busting literary classic. It charts the life of Stephen, an upper class young woman who finds love in the arms of Mary, an older ambulance driver, only for the pair to suffer isolation and rejection from a cruel world. Hall hoped it might encourage a 'more tolerant understanding' of queer people, and thought she had 'put [her] pen at the service of some of the most persecuted and misunderstood people in the world.' It didn't go down well. Deemed a 'danger to the nation', Hall's novel was banned four months after publication, after medical advice that it could lead women to become lesbians. It was finally released in 1949.

Born in 1880 to wealth and privilege, Hall's status allowed her a certain eccentricity: what we might read as fantastically queer today was nothing more than fascinatingly odd at the time. Hall dressed in men's clothing (she wore a leather riding coat and Spanish riding hat to *The Well*'s censorship court case), called herself 'John', lived with her female partner Una Troubridge, and appeared in photographs and artworks in her bespoke, masculine finery. *The Well* was a risk, however; it might have exposed Hall and Una as lesbians, but she felt compelled to publish it. Una and Hall stayed together until Hall's death in 1943, leaving a legacy of gender-bending imagery and the world's most influential lesbian tragic novel.

Gladys Bentley

To Harry Hansberry's Clam House, Manhattan, the tiny 1920s gay speakeasy where larger-than-life blues performer Gladys Bentley (1907–1960) sang her way to fame. Big, black, openly gay, dressed up in men's clothes, Bentley was an unlikely star of the shadowy Prohibition underworld.

Moving from Philadelphia to Harlem when she was 16, Bentley found herself slap bang in a burgeoning artistic and free-living African-American community. It was also New York's epicentre of vice; its network of speakeasies was the perfect place to drink a Top & Bottom (gin and wine), smoke weed, attend drag balls, and see the greatest, naughtiest talents perform. By the late '20s, Bentley had recorded a number of 78s, had a radio show, and found her notoriety allowed her to wear whatever she liked: usually a tux and top hat. In the early '30s she upgraded, headlining at swankier clubs backed by a posse of drag queens, but it was in 1931 that things got really interesting. Rumours abounded that Bentley had got hitched to a white woman in a civil ceremony in New Jersey – decades before same sex marriage was legalised.

So far, so queer, but in a 1954 article in *Ebony* magazine, Bentley attempted to destroy her gay persona. Suddenly, she was cured of 'her strange affliction', had married a man, and appeared in a photo shoot doing household chores. What had become of this lioness of a woman? Had the puritanism of the McCarthy era force her to put on another costume, that of a clean-living, dutiful wife? Or perhaps Bentley was showing she still had the energy to shock, provoke and mystify, right up to her death in 1960.

kd lang

'Elvis is alive, and she's beautiful,' said Madonna (see page 80) of kd lang (Kathryn Dawn Lang; born 1961). It was the height of lang's fame and the handsome Canadian with the sensuous, Patsy Cline drawl was, quite simply, the world's most famous lesbian. In the mid '90s, the quiet country singer – and queer culture itself – was having a bit of a moment. lang's *Ingénue* (1992), her multi-million-selling, Grammy-nominated album, saw her draped in supermodels and celebs, attending fashion shows, falling out of boozy parties – even shot by Herb Ritts for the cover of *Vanity Fair* (1993) being shaved by Cindy Crawford.

lang grew up on the prairie lands of Edmonton and formed a band, The Reclines, in 1983. She worked her own brand of 'cowboy punk' in kitsch outfits, started picking up awards, and recorded 'Crying', a duet with Roy Orbison, in 1987. She then starred in queer cult classic *Salmonberries* (1991), and the legendary coming-out episode of *Ellen* (1997).

At the height of her fame, lang ran the cool kids: she counted actor and comedian Sandra Bernhard (see page 66) and Madonna as friends, and 'lesbian chic' was a thing. After *Ingénue*, she used her new star power to become a spokesperson for lesbian and gay issues, animal rights, and human rights in Tibet. Although the press has stopped frothing about lang (and the huge gains made in the '90s towards the visibility of gay people in mainstream media have proved a little fickle), the effect lang and her music had on a generation of queer kids should not be underestimated.

Camille Paglia

Camille Paglia (born 1947) is an unstoppable force. The academic, critic, and all-round queer badass rips apart social theories, devours pop culture icons, and destroys the hallowed works of her contemporaries – nothing and no one is untouchable. Just watch her in action: her energetic, rapid-fire discourse reveals a brain fizzing with ideas, cryptic references, wry jokes – and she leaves very few gaps for questions.

Paglia graduated from Binghamton University, New York, in 1968 as valedictorian (even though she had proudly been on probation for a series of pranks), and is thought to be the first openly gay woman at Yale Graduate School from 1968–72. Finding her voice, she developed new theories of sexual history, popular culture, and art, and continued to argue with her idols, leaving her first teaching post after a period of intense feather-ruffling. Paglia became a professor at the University of Arts in Philadelphia in 1984, and has been one of academia's strongest, loudest voices ever since. Her writing is camp, comic, and salacious; pro-sex, art, fashion, beauty, and Hollywood; and her explosive book *Sexual Personae* (1990) made sure she was at the centre of the culture wars of the '90s.

Today, Paglia remains at odds with contemporary feminism and is searingly blunt with her criticism. Her academic legacy? Ultimately, she perceives herself a truth-teller; a champion of free-thinking and the independent mind, and her ideas continue to be impassioned and divisive. She is as wonderfully loud-mouthed as ever.

Keith Haring

Gawky art hero Keith Haring (1958–90) is the bespectacled sub-way scrawler whose cartoonish drawings of birth, death, love, sex and freedom became synonymous with the creative renaissance of 1980s New York. Through hundreds of works created in white chalk across the NYC transport system and beyond, Haring's raw, vibrant style marked him out as a queer, sex-positive artist who dealt in social justice.

Haring moved to New York City in 1978, enrolled at the School of Visual Arts, and soon discovered a growing grungy, alt-art com-munity on the Lower East Side. Befriending artists like Jean-Michel Basquiat, as well as graffiti writers, and performers like Fab 5 Freddy and Madonna (see page 80), Haring became a major figure on the scene, organising group exhibitions and happenings. Four years after arriving in New York, Haring's first major show attracted the likes of Andy Warhol (see page 58) and Roy Lichtenstein.

It was the subway where Haring developed his art. His crawling 'radiant' babies, UFOs and spiky-toothed dogs became a familiar sight for commuting New Yorkers, and Haring became increasingly dedicated to public art, accessible to all. Soon, he was travelling the world creating new works for hospitals, children's centres and charities, and took part in more than 100 solo and group exhibitions.

In 1988, Haring was diagnosed with Aids and the following year set up the Keith Haring Foundation to provide funding and artworks to Aids organisations. He died one year later at the age of 31.

Haring's imagery played a huge part in the activism and aware-ness surrounding Aids. To this day, his foundation supports not-for-profits that help under-privileged children and organisations that focus on Aids education, prevention and care.

Barbara Gittings

Barbara Gittings (1932–2007) is the civil rights pioneer who, with her partner, Kay Tobin Lahusen (the first gay photojournalist), campaigned for gay equality for almost 46 years, founding the first ever national lesbian organisation and coming out in the couple's assisted-living facility newsletter.

In the late 1950s, very few gay people came out, but Gittings didn't get the memo. She was a highly visible, passionate and militant lesbian activist who founded the New York chapter of the Daughters of Bilitis and edited *The Ladder*, the nation's first lesbian rag, from 1963–66. She was at early gay rights demos at the White House in the '60s to end discrimination against gay people in federal employment. And in the early '70s, Gittings helped lobby the American Psychiatric Association, protesting at meetings, grabbing the microphone, and eventually appearing on panels arguing that the APA should remove its definition of homosexuality as a mental disorder (she succeeded in 1973).

Almost always on the front line, Gittings worked hard in the background too: she campaigned for public libraries to increase information about gay life, inspired by the lack thereof when she was growing up. As a teenager, her father caught her reading Radclyffe Hall's (see page 14) *The Well of Loneliness* (and promptly asked her to burn it), but there was little else in libraries to help or inspire her. She set about changing all that.

For many, Gittings is the grande dame of the modern LGBT+ rights movement. In their seventies, Gittings and Lahusen moved into an assisted-living apartment, and one of their last acts was to come out in the centre's newsletter. Gittings remained outspoken, proud of who she was, right until the end.

RuPaul

'If you can't love yourself, how the hell are you gonna love somebody else?' asks the bewigged RuPaul (born 1960), the iconic ex-punk cover girl and shrewd owner of a media empire. The world's most famous drag queen is a steely, often hilarious creation who only dresses up when the price is right.

Growing up in San Diego, RuPaul struggled with being different. He had a dark period as a teenage misfit, but with the support of his family, he knew his tribe was out there. At 15, he moved with his sister to Atlanta, Georgia, to study performing arts. There, he found himself submerged in the underground cinema and punk music scene (with a little dancing on the side). But it was in the mid '80s that he moved from Atlanta to New York, stepped his impossibly long legs into a frock, and became a superstar. You can spot him in the B-52s' *Love Shack* video (1989), and soon he had his own pop mega-hit with *Supermodel (You Better Work)* (1992). Later, he hosted a chat show, performed a duet with Elton, hung out with Kurt Cobain and Courtney Love – and became the first male face of MAC Cosmetics.

In 2009, he debuted *RuPaul's Drag Race*, a slightly shoddy, low-budget TV commission that mocked the format of model reality shows. Fledgling drag queens compete for the top spot in a sequin-studded bun fight that makes for compulsive viewing. The not-so-secret subtext of the show is to reveal the difficult lives of the men who take part in it, many of whom have been kicked out of home or struggle to make ends meet. The series won an Emmy in 2016.

RuPaul is always busy, launching a make-up line, recording albums, and teaching straight white America the filthiest drag slang imaginable. 'You better work' is a slogan to live by, it seems. So, to what does he owe his success? 'Kindness only goes so far,' says Ru, 'and then it's time to show your claws.'

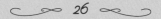

Chavela Vargas

There are many thrilling and salacious rumours about the life of Latin American icon and Mexican chanteuse, Chavela Vargas (1919–2012). There's the one about her singing at Liz Taylor's wedding in Acapulco and bedding Ava Gardner after the reception, or the moment Frida Kahlo (see page 106) told her 'I live only for you and Diego.' Each story paints Vargas' vocal (and sexual) career as a rollercoaster ride through decades of celebrity lesbianism – a life lived big.

Born in Costa Rica, Isabel Vargas Lizano moved to Mexico when she was 14 (she sold chickens for the bus fare), hoping to make it as a singer. For years, she performed on the streets, dressed in men's clothes and wielding a gun, singing Mexican *rancheras* traditionally sung by men. She was discovered in the 1950s by songwriter José Alfredo Jiménez, who supported the release of her first album. Vargas had fallen in with an influential, arty set that saw her fame grow throughout the '60s and '70s. She recorded more than 80 albums, toured Europe and the States, and knocked back a huge amount of tequila. She came out when she was 81 years old.

In her later years, Vargas would tell how she was tormented by others because of her sexuality; her rich, dark and deep voice was edged with pain. She transformed old, camp songs into works of art, refused to change the gender of famous love songs to croon obediently to men, and in the '70s, many of Vargas' songs became queer anthems. A muse of Pedro Almodóvar, it was the Spanish director who encouraged Vargas to play her biggest, most impressive venue yet – Carnegie Hall, NYC – and in 2003 she did just that. Not bad for a queer, gun-toting singer who took her first steps to fame on the city streets.

Rock Hudson

Rock Hudson (1925–85) is the impossibly handsome screen idol of Hollywood's golden age who – like many of his contemporaries – infamously hid his sexuality from plain sight.

Director Douglas Sirk gave Hudson his first starring role in *Magnificent Obsession* (1954) but his star power became obvious after the release of *Giant* (1956) which scored him an Oscar nomination. Hudson's carefully crafted celeb persona was pure box-office gold: he was tall and broad-chested, with a superhero's jawline, a deep, masculine voice, and a sense of humour. Studios were careful to cast him in tough-yet-sensitive roles. He was the perfect heart-throb, romantically linked to any number of glamourous Hollywood women, and caused hearts to flutter and knickers to fizz all over the world. Yet, when Hudson's sexuality was eventually revealed, the true construction of his on-screen character was laid bare.

Hudson was, in part, the creation of Henry Willson, and one of a long line of (mainly gay) men the uber-agent deftly rebuilt and renamed, from Tab Hunter to Dack Rambo. Each was given a manly resume and schooled in the art of acting straight, but it was Hudson through which Willson had his greatest success.

Later in his career, Hudson appeared in a handful of films, but by the early '80s, his health had deteriorated. Then came a turning point: in 1985, Hudson announced he had HIV. The idea that a beloved national treasure like Hudson could have Aids was a huge shock, but Hudson's bravery in finally speaking out helped de-stigmatise the illness, and opened up a dialogue about what it meant to be gay in contemporary America. He died the same year.

 31

James Baldwin

James Baldwin (1924–87) is the late, great American queer writer, essayist, and social commentator. To many, he was the voice of the American civil rights struggle of the late '50s and '60s. As his contemporaries like Malcolm X, Martin Luther King, and activist Medgar Evers were murdered, and a bomb blasted through a church in Alabama, his was one of the loudest, angriest screams against racism.

Baldwin grew up in Harlem. He excelled at school, loved writing, and was mentored by black Greenwich Village painter Beauford Delaney, who helped Baldwin realise a black person could be an artist. So, he wrote. At 24, he escaped New York and its woeful opportunities for black men, and moved to France. He published his first novel *Go Tell It on the Mountain* in 1953 and his essays *Notes from a Native Son* appeared two years later. Then came *Giovanni's Room* (1956), a study of gay shame and malaise across the bars and backrooms of Paris.

Baldwin was completely uncompromising. White pro-equality liberals found his anger – incandescent at times – shocking. And black activists found Baldwin a problematic ally: he criticised black Christian culture, attacked the literary works of his forebears, and his queerness set him apart in a civil rights movement that was often hostile towards gay people. Readers who expected him to write about the African-American experience found Baldwin's friendship with establishment figures like Norman Mailer, and works like *Giovanni's Room* with its white gay characters, a little unsettling.

Throughout his life, Baldwin remained steadfast in his beliefs, and was completely open about his queerness, however uncomfortable that made others. Most of all, he was a gifted writer, flamboyant one minute, and delicately nuanced the next. With its themes of race, sexuality, and alienation, his work has taken on a peculiar poignancy in modern times.

Lili Elbe

Lili Elbe (1882–1931) is the Danish artist and gender pioneer whose brave social and physical transformation and frank personal diaries have inspired others across the decades.

Known as Einar Mogens Wegener, the tenacious and ambitious teenage boy swapped a sleepy fjord-side village to study at the Royal Danish Academy of Fine Arts in Copenhagen. It was there Einar fell for fellow artist Gerda Gottlieb – the pair married in 1904 – and their life together was full of colour, art, and rather fancy dresses.

Privately, Einar would model women's clothing for Gerda's high-fashion illustrations, and her subsequent works offered a glimpse into another world, a world where she was a woman. The pair moved to Paris in 1912 and, after years trying to suppress the inner identity Einar named Lili, Paris seemed the perfect place to transition into her true self. Lili finally stepped out of the shadows and, with Gerda, into the nightlife of upscale Paris society.

In the 1920s, Lili discovered the possibility of surgically altering her body at the German Institute for Sexual Science in Berlin. The term 'transsexualism' was coined by the clinic's founder, gay rights activist Dr Magnus Hirschfeld. Lili underwent a series of pioneering operations both at the Institute and at the Dresden clinic of Kurt Warnekros (a man she described as her 'saviour') in 1930–31.

Yet, as Lili blossomed, her old life began to unravel. Friends rejected her, she was granted a divorce, and her family desperately missed Einar, their beloved brother and son. She became untethered to the past and struggled to find acceptance. A final operation ended her life in September 1931. Earlier that summer, Lili had written to a friend. 'That I, Lili, am vital and have a right to life I have proved by living for 14 months,' she explained. 'It may be said that 14 months is not much, but they seem to me like a whole and happy human life.'

Quentin Crisp

All suburbanites dream of escape, and Quentin Crisp (1908–99) was no exception. Born Denis Pratt, he set about reinventing himself into a refined, pastel-hued queer creature of the likes unseen on the streets of south London. A little lipstick here, a dab of nail polish there, and a new, impossibly fey-sounding name marked Crisp out as something of a gender pioneer of the time.

In his twenties, Crisp struggled to hold down a job, studying journalism and art and, through hanging out in the cafes of Soho, became a sex worker, too. He entertained London's 'brightest and roughest' (according to his diaries) from his tiny flat and worked on sharpening his wit. Escaping conscription because of 'sexual perversion', Crisp loved wartime London and his affection for US culture apparently stemmed from his night-time fumbles with American GIs. His notoriety grew; Crisp published three short books and by 1968 he was the subject of a documentary, but it was the 1975 film adaptation of Crisp's *The Naked Civil Servant* starring John Hurt that secured the raconteur's stardom. He toured a show about his life and moved to New York in 1981, listing his name in the telephone directory so he could accept any invitation he received, from dinners (he loved a free meal) to film appearances.

Crisp's soft, floppy-hatted exterior and delicate mauve hair belied a shrewd wit and somewhat dark ideals. He loved to be controversial; he made people laugh, but furiously angry, too. He seemed at odds with contemporary gay liberation rhetoric, and when challenged, hardened his views. In his final years, he failed to grasp the shift in attitudes towards queer civil equality; to him, the Aids crisis was 'a fad', and gay men had 'feminine minds'. Yet, he stuck to his guns. There had always been something immovable about Crisp and it took unbelievable courage to walk the streets of 1920s London as his true, flamboyant self. He was a man who refused to be anyone else.

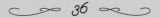

Gertrude Stein

Was Gertrude Stein (1874–1946) the original Mean Girl? The Parisian apartment she shared with her partner Alice B Toklas was the gossipy hangout of intellectual thought in mid-century Europe. An off-hand remark from Stein – delivered from under a blunt, pudding-bowl haircut – could make or break an artist's reputation.

Stein was something of a genius-collector. The writer, novelist, playwright and art collector moved to Paris from Pennsylvania in 1903 in pursuit of the finest minds in Europe, and it was there she met San Franciscan expat Alice in 1906. They soon shacked up and did whatever pleased them, filling their apartment with good food, artists and writers, and refused to do anything that didn't suit them. To that end, they were openly, and rather bravely, gay (more than a little eyebrow-raising in the early 1900s).

Stein's manly gait and Toklas' wispy 'tache deftly challenged notions of feminine beauty (the story of Stein's little nephew exclaiming after the pair's visit that he liked the man, 'but why did the woman have a moustache?' is a somewhat cheeky illustration of this).

Although she had written throughout her adult life (works the average reader strains to understand), in was in 1933 that Stein shot to wider acclaim with her best-selling novel *The Autobiography of Alice B Toklas* (written in Toklas' voice).

In many ways, Stein and Toklas were brilliantly gender nonconforming, but they seemed to live a rather traditional hetero lifestyle. Artists and writers like Pablo Picasso, Ernest Hemingway, F Scott Fitzgerald and Henri Matisse would come seeking audience with Stein, while their wives sat dutifully with Toklas. And yet, it worked. The pair are still considered the dynamic intellectual duo of that era; two women who most definitely had it their way.

Harvey Milk

To 1970s San Francisco and the gay days of handlebar moustaches, steamy bath houses, macramé, and angry, full-blooded street protest. Ultimate queer hero, Harvey Milk (1930–78), was the passionate local business-owner-turned-politician who became the first openly gay person elected to public office in California.

Although San Francisco was the epicentre of alternative culture in the US, and the Castro District the spiritual home of queer life, a staunch, religiously-motivated national conservatism hung over the growing gay community. Angry with the entrapment of local gay people, heavy-handed police persecution, and laws limiting the rights of LGBT citizens, Milk decided to run for office.

Winning over hearts and minds with his frankness and humour, Milk's dogged rise to power employed the tactical genius of firing up gay voters, forming surprising coalitions, and promising to sort out San Francisco's chihuahua poop problem. In 1977, on his third attempt, he finally scored a place on the Board of Supervisors. He burned brightly. In his 11-month reign, he was the driving force behind a gay-rights law that prohibited discrimination, spearheaded programmes to benefit minority groups and the elderly, and helped defeat a state senate proposal to prohibit gay people teaching in public schools in California.

On 27 November, 1978, Milk and Mayor Moscone were shot dead by disgruntled former city supervisor, Dan White. At trial, White was found guilty only of voluntary manslaughter, escaping a harsh murder sentence. Furious Milk supporters took part in the city's infamous White Night riots. The following night, thousands took to Castro Street for another reason: to celebrate what would have been Milk's 49th birthday.

Patricia Highsmith

In 1952, using the pseudonym Claire Morgan, Patricia Highsmith (1921–95), published a work of fiction the likes of which the world had never seen: a sexy, heart-breaking lesbian novel with a happy ending. In *The Price of Salt*, the gay American novelist and short story writer – whose works are considered the finest, most nail-biting example of suspense lit – drew on her own sultry entanglements with former lovers in the glamourous 1950s Greenwich Village.

Born in Texas, Highsmith maintained a lifelong love-hate relationship with her mother (who died just four years before Highsmith). Graduating from women's liberal arts college Barnard in 1942, Highsmith wrote short stories and comics, and struggled to secure a job in journalism. Encouraged by Truman Capote, in 1948 Highsmith gained a place on the Yaddo arts retreat where she worked on her first novel, the best-selling *Strangers on a Train* (1950). A year later, Hitchcock released the movie version – a smash hit. Not bad for a debut novelist.

'The poet of apprehension' is how Graham Greene once described Highsmith's writing, but this seemed to be true socially, too. She was a mercurial dinner guest, dry and funny one minute, and cruel the next. Biographers talk of trouble with alcohol and depression, and an inability to have long-term relationships, but Highsmith's output was consistently impressive. She wrote more than 20 novels, inspiring big-budget movie adaptations, created iconic characters like Tom Ripley, and apparently had time to break hearts across New York.

The Price of Salt was inspired by an icy blonde woman in a mink whom Highsmith spotted while working at Bloomingdales as a young shop girl, much like the character Therese in the novel. Thirty-eight years after its debut, near the end of Highsmith's life, the world had changed. Highsmith decided that *Salt*, her most personal novel, be republished as *Carol* (1990), but this time under her real name.

Peter Tatchell

Peter Tatchell (born 1952) is outrageous. For decades he's interrupted political speeches, organised kiss-ins and sit-ins inside anti-gay pubs, invaded a pulpit to protest the Archbishop of Canterbury's attitude towards gay people, and performed a citizen's arrest on a furious Robert Mugabe. And with Outrage!, the queer equality pressure group, Tatchell shockingly helped to 'out' ten bishops who were accused of condemning homosexuality in public while living secretly gay lives. Tatchell is not only outrageous, but he goes where others fear to tread.

Born in Australia, Tatchell has been a campaigner for human rights all his adult life. When he was just 19, he moved to London and joined the Gay Liberation Front, taking part in protests against police brutality, and helping organise the city's first Pride march in 1972. In the '90s, Outrage! became notorious as one of the world's most headline-grabbing non-violent direct action groups, and Tatchell's name soon became synonymous with protest.

There's no end to Tatchell's energy, or the tricky situations he'll put himself through in the name of human rights, from challenging ultra-right-wing groups to campaigning on the streets for LGBT-Muslim solidarity. Yet, there's a nasty side effect to his work: he's survived countless physical attacks, suffering vicious beatings from Mugabe's bodyguards in 2001 and the Moscow police in 2007.

Over the years, Tatchell's relentlessness has worn down the establishment and he's achieved a begrudging affection and acceptance from many of the institutions he has criticised. And his self-titled human rights foundation does great work (it's the perfect platform for this fantastically unstoppable loudmouth). Tatchell is constantly warned about saying the wrong thing and alienating those who might be allies – 'Why can't he just toe the line?' – but as long as he starts a conversation, he knows he might just achieve something wonderful.

Sylvia Rivera

On a hot, sticky June night in 1969 in New York City, after years of harassment and fear, an army of drag queens fought back against a police raid at the Stonewall Inn. The riot is considered the beginning of the modern LGBT+ rights movement, and – although exact details of that night are a little hazy – it seems it was Sylvia Rivera (1951–2002) who lead the charge.

Rivera's childhood, much of it undocumented, was horrific. She lost her mother to suicide and by the age of 10 or 11 was on her own in Times Square. She was a sex worker, lived as a trans woman, and was an activist who risked everything – violence, arrest, her own safety – to play her part in the LGBT+ story.

Rivera founded Star (Street Transvestite Action Revolutionaries) with fellow activist Marsha P Johnson, and opened a homeless shelter for transgender youth. She was a passionate advocate for civil equality, but her volatile nature often put her at odds with those she wished to align with. She found herself caught between gay libbers and the women's movement, struggling to find real acceptance in either group. In 1973, she was booed off stage at a rally in Washington Square Park for her angry words towards the gay community for failing to accept difference within its ranks.

Rivera wouldn't back down. Today, many credit Rivera's years of activism for opening the queer movement up to be more inclusive, to embrace people of colour, gender non-conformists, people of different economic backgrounds, and trans people. A fitting legacy for a unique woman.

47

Justin Vivian Bond

Award-winning performer, artist, writer, and activist Justin Vivian Bond (born 1963) has sparkled in the spotlight for more than three decades. Crooning in smoky dive bars, draped across a piano wailing out *Smells Like Teen Spirit* or *Space Oddity*, Bond's husky, gin-soaked creation Kiki DuRane became a cult figure on the '90s and '00s cabaret circuit as one half of award-winning act Kiki & Herb. Cult indie movies, solo art shows, and a book followed. Over the years, Bond has cultivated an influential body of work, from writing to original music – even a fragrance.

Growing up trans in the Maryland suburbs of the 1970s, Bond seemed to defy gender norms with every step, every utterance. As a young boy who wore frosted pink lipstick to school (Iced Watermelon by Revlon, FYI), Bond twirled like Fred and Ginger, hoping to be both, fooled around with local boys, and came of age in the crosshairs of bullies and a conservative family. If Bond's autobiography *Tango: My Childhood, Backwards and in High Heels* (2011) reveals a child who danced right up to the boundaries of gender, as an adult, Bond has foxtrotted over them entirely.

As a trailblazer of trans expression, non-binary language and new pronouns (Bond prefers 'mx' and 'v'), and champion of feminism and civil rights, Bond cuts a persuasive, eloquent figure. Self-described as a 'trans-genre' artist – a nifty term, ripe with meaning, yet open to interpretation – Bond has an almost indefinable quality. There's the political satirist, the accomplished artist, and the passionate activist. But there's also lipstick and glitter, lonesome love songs, and just a little bit of magic.

49

Virginia Woolf

'Women alone stir my imagination,' wrote Britain's most celebrated modernist writer in 1930, sending literary critics, queer historians, and bookish lesbian undergrads aquiver for decades afterwards.

In the 1970s, in the light of feminist literary criticism, the work of Virginia Woolf (1882–1941) was feverishly re-examined. A Woolf pack of academic super-fans uncovered gay eroticism, contemporary feminist thought, and a steamy love affair between the novelist and her friend Vita Sackville-West.

Woolf was born into Victorian London literati. Her father, Sir Leslie Stephen, was an author and critic; her sister, Vanessa Bell, an accomplished painter; and writers like Henry James would drop by for tea. In 1904, Woolf, her sister Vanessa and brother Thoby hot-footed to London's Bloomsbury where they formed what came to be known as the Bloomsbury Group, a gang of precocious and brilliant queer and queer-friendly creatives and pranksters, from EM Forster to Woolf's future husband, Leonard.

Woolf wrote 10 novels, numerous essays and short stories in her lifetime, from *To the Lighthouse* (1927) to *Orlando* (1928), a tale of a woman who flips genders, inspired by Sackville-West's life. Woolf also helped set up the legendary book publisher, the Hogarth Press. Letters between Woolf and Sackville-West seem to reveal the pair were in open marriages, and it is thought their partners were also bisexual: a situation completely at odds with Victorian society of the time. Woolf is not just a hero of literary modernism, but sexual modernism, too.

George Takei

Set phasers to stun: George Takei (born 1937) is the galaxy-hopping Japanese American actor, writer, director and *bon vivant* whose adventures to the outer reaches of the universe, years of activism and sassy online takedowns have made him an intergalactic treasure.

Born in LA, Takei was imprisoned with his family in 1942 in a series of internment camps in California and Arkansas until the end of World War II. The experience left an indelible mark on him. He studied architecture but, like so many other Angelinos, ended up in the movies, and by the late '50s he had played bit parts in blockbuster films and TV dramas. But it was *Star Trek* (1966) that made him a star. The series deftly used camp, wobbly sci-fi to reflect the social issues of the time, from civil rights and racial and gender equality to the futility of war – and Takei, as Lieutenant Sulu, was literally at the helm.

By the 1970s, Takei had decided to use his celebrity to speak out about further causes close to his heart, starting with post-internment Japanese-American relations and most recently taking on queer issues. Takei was closeted for most of his adult life, but all that changed after Governor of California Arnold Schwarzenegger vetoed the state's marriage equality bill. Takei was incensed, and decided to finally come out in 2005, thinking it would surely be the end of his career. He couldn't have been more wrong.

Takei is arguably more famous now than at any point in his career (his social media stats are out of this solar system), and maintains an elegant yet deadly wit, churning out daily bon mots and thrillingly acerbic social commentary. It's as if after those years of hiding away, his true thoughts and feelings have come out at once – and the universe is all the better for it.

Jake Miller

Jake Miller (born 1972) is the muscle-bound motivational speaker, trans activist, filmmaker and actor whose rascally alter-ego, Buck Angel, has appeared in hundreds of eye-popping adult movies (perhaps don't Google it at work). His aim? To eroticise the trans body, increase visibility, and explore the ins and outs of trans male identity.

At school, Miller (then known as Susan) found it hard to fit in, and his journey to transitioning was a difficult one. Testosterone therapy and top surgery followed and Miller started to work on his physique and buffed up. Then came adult movies. Miller was working behind the scenes, building websites, wondering why there were no transgender men in porn. He decided to change that. No one had seen anything like Buck Angel before and at first, Miller's tattooed on-screen creation found it hard to carve a niche in the industry. But soon, Angel had his own following and his fame grew.

In 2012, Miller's work began to evolve from making sweaty, sexy cult movies to education. He now speaks at events around the world, giving his views on human sexuality, gender, and how wider society perceives non-binary and trans people, along with safe sex advice and feminist perspectives on pornography. And his online documentary series *Sexing the Transman* (2011) gives a further voice to trans men and their relationship with sex, all in a lo-fi adult movie format.

Miller's work – both his adult movies and trans education drive – is unique. It's a careful balancing act to maintain Buck Angel's naughtiness with Miller's own progressive aims, but he enjoys subverting expectations. As he loves to say: 'It's not what's between your legs that defines you.'

Sally Ride

Lesbians are everywhere – even in space. Sally Ride (1951–2012) is the physicist, science educator, and first American woman to fly in space. A national treasure, her obituary revealed something previously unknown to an adoring public: for 27 years, she had shared her life with Dr Tam O'Shaughnessy, a woman.

In 1977, NASA began a recruitment drive for female astronauts. Ride was still a student at Stanford and spotted an ad in the school newspaper. She applied for the job, became one of six women picked to join the program, and on 18 June, 1983, she blasted off on a space shuttle mission working a robotic arm to install satellites. She flew on the space shuttle again in 1984. At first, the press weren't quite sure what to make of a female astronaut (hilariously, she was asked if she got moody when things didn't go right in training), but they were soon won over.

Sally and Tam met when they were girls; they were lifelong friends but became partners in 1985 (Ride divorced her husband, a fellow astronaut, in 1987). They co-authored books together and helped run Sally Ride Science, Ride's organisation to make science fun and accessible to the young (girls in particular).

As the first American woman in space, there was huge expectation on Ride, and she felt it acutely. An intensely private person, she never spoke publicly about her relationship with Tam, but socially – to friends, family, and colleagues – they were known as a loving couple. Tam is now Executive Director of Sally Ride Science (now a non-profit at The University of California, San Diego). There, she carries on Sally's work, the woman who went to the stars.

Andy Warhol

Andy Warhol (1928–87) is the American artist who lorded over a court of legendary creatives, musicians, models, celebrities, drag queens and oddballs in 1960s, '70s and '80s New York City. His official legacy is an impossibly vast collection of films, video, drawings, screen prints and sculpture; *Interview* magazine; the Velvet Underground; album covers; books; and hilariously sharp-tongued diaries. Then there are the wonderfully weird time capsules: approximately 600 boxed and filed letters, objects and ephemera, and 30 ghostly silver-white wigs. But it's a near indefinable thing that marks Warhol out as a queer hero: his work was to underline others' sexuality rather than his own, to swing the spotlight away from his shy, Pennsylvanian persona and onto the drag stars, punk girls, leather boys and handsome hustlers that hung out at the original Silver Factory.

For those who document Warhol's own sexuality, one conclusion is usually reached: it's complicated. He balanced Ruthenian Catholicism with being an openly gay man, and shocked with films like *Blow Job* (1964) and *Taylor Mead's Ass* (1965) that implied a life of debauchery (even though he liked to watch from the sidelines and was usually in bed by 10 pm). At a time when his fame was absolute, Warhol's work unveiled and celebrated a queer underworld that was previously unknown.

In 1968, Warhol survived a murder attempt that left him with lifelong medical problems. The Factory increased security, stalling the creative freedom the Warhol set had enjoyed for almost a decade. When he died in 1987, Warhol left behind artworks and artifacts that seem to scream their queerness, but his own true wants remain hidden between the lines.

Billie Holiday

Billie Holiday (1915–59) lived a life of extremes. As the iconic vocalist of evocative, heart-wrenching jazz and blues standards, she balanced joy and fame precariously with the tragedy of her youth. The singer of *Strange Fruit* (1939) (the bitter depiction of a lynching) had a troubled upbringing: a cycle of abuse, neglect and poverty that seemed impossible to escape.

Born Eleanora Fagan to a 13-year-old mother, the pair travelled to New York in 1928. Eleanora sang at a club in Harlem, performing six nights a week, and changed her name to Billie Holiday. She was introduced to Benny Goodman, started recording, and her fame grew. A one-woman residency at Café Society followed, and it was there that Billie put together her trademark look: bright red lips and white gardenias in her hair, her fingers snapping along Sinatra-like to the rhythm.

Holiday often had strained relationships with men, but her friendship with actress Tallulah Bankhead was the source of much gossip. Like fellow jazz greats Ma Rainey and Bessie Smith, Holiday was bisexual and had a number of steamy relationships with other women. Bankhead would come to Holiday's shows, follow her on tour, and even bailed her out of jail after she had been arrested for opium possession. Holiday fans love to pore over the furious letters the two sent each other after Billie's autobiography came out. In the clubland of 1930s and '40s New York, hiding one's sexuality wasn't always necessary, and although it had an element of danger, Holiday's love of women wasn't a secret from her peers. Known affectionately as Lady Day, her legacy is a wealth of emotionally frayed songs and a voice that has inspired countless modern artists.

Dan Savage

Need to get off? Then you need Dan Savage (born 1964). For more than 25 years, his iconic sex advice column, *Savage Love*, has helped Americans – gay, straight, and in-between – understand and accept their wildest urges, from cheesy foot fetishes and hairy nipple worship to tickling, peeing, and sploshing. What's more, he flies the flag for LGBT+ civil equality, fighting the queer corner on any platform that will have him, and mauling his opponents with lightning-fast wit, humour, and outrage.

Savage Love first appeared in Seattle's *The Stranger* in 1991. Savage was angry. It was the height of the Aids crisis; his friends were dying and no one seemed to care. He set out to create a column that was as contemptuous of straight people and straight sex as other advice columns had been towards gay people and gay sex. Only it backfired: straight people loved his furious, tell-it-like-it-is tone, and Savage garnered a surprise following of straight men who used his column, and later, phone-in podcast, as an outlet for miserable sex lives, 'Am I gay?' worries, and the venting of sticky unfulfilled desires.

Savage grew up in a staunchly Catholic household. His mother was a lay minister, his father a deacon, and – as Savage points out – the bravery needed to tell his family he was gay at the age of 17 rendered him more or less unshockable. In fact, he is refreshingly open about his own life experience: happy to discuss his marriage, fatherhood (Savage and his husband Terry have a son, DJ), the loss of his virginity (in a tent with his brother's ex-girlfriend and another man, dressed in medieval costume) and his own peccadillos and passions, from politics to leather. It follows that Savage has his opponents, from right wing politicos to frothing religious fundamentalists who see him, and everything he stands for, as the symbol of modern moral decay. Savage would think they just weren't getting any.

 63

Audre Lorde

Just before her death, poet, feminist, activist, and 'crazy and queer' hero Audre Lorde (1934–92) took a new name in an African naming ceremony. She became Gamba Adisa, meaning Warrior: She Who Makes Her Meaning Known. In the final throes of cancer, she had spent a lifetime defining meaning, not just for herself, but for the others who loved her angry poetry and emotional (and rather sexy) prose. She unpicked the fabric of race, gender and sexuality, and sought to make something that had not existed before. 'I started writing,' she said, 'because I had a need inside of me to create something that was not there.'

Lorde was born in New York into the kind of tricky family dynamics needed to be a truly wonderful writer: her light-skinned mother was distrustful of her daughter's own darker skin and her father was cold and distant. As a writer and performer, Lorde was deadly serious one minute, and light and coquettish the next. Today, she might be read as an intersectional feminist – holding the belief that oppressive institutions (such as racism or sexism) are interconnected and cannot be examined individually. Lorde was dogged in the fighting of all prejudice, not only in mainstream culture, but within feminism, too. Her techniques were powerful, from the unapologetic way she might underline her identity as a 'black feminist lesbian mother poet' in readings and debates, to how she might split up her usually all-female audiences, asking black women to stay after a performance and introduce themselves, forging new relationships.

In 1984, Lorde moved to Berlin; racism in Europe, specifically Germany, became a flashpoint in her work, but she loved the city and the vitality of the German women's movement. She felt free. After she died, Lorde left a legacy of writing, readings and debates that sought to uncover the truth about the way we live. Using sunshine as disinfectant, Audre Lorde's words let in the light.

Sandra Bernhard

Sandra Bernhard (born 1955) is the gangly American performer, author and activist who came to fame in the 1970s with her searing stand-up shows, cutting through the hairy-balled comedy fraternity with a brash, female skew. In between the punchlines, Bernhard is known for being furiously 'outspoken' (something her male counterparts might not be charged with), but it's a quality that has made her stand out as a hugely creative and political talent.

In 1977, Bernhard's stand-up act scored her a place on *The Richard Pryor Show*, but it was in 1983 that she shot to fame in Scorsese's *The King of Comedy* as Masha, a suitably creepy stalker. A slew of one-woman shows followed and Bernhard's star was in the ascendant. It's best not to define Bernhard through her friendship with one-time gal pal Madonna (see page 80), but it was that – and rumours of a relationship – which excited the tabloid press and pushed Bernhard's celebrity ever further.

Bernhard has a daughter with her longtime female partner, is a vocal supporter of gay equality, and broke new ground playing Nancy in *Roseanne*, one of the first lesbian characters in a prime-time sitcom. In the early '90s she took somewhat of an unexpected turn, popping up in *Playboy*, but then hit big on Broadway with another stand-up show, critiquing the great and good of the worlds of politics and celebrity. Bernhard is at her best when she lays into lofty untouchables, pointing out hypocrisy with humour and buckets of personality. She has always been a risk-taker in ways most contemporary comics are not, and she doesn't care if you're offended. Just the way it should be.

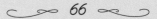

67

Essex Hemphill

Essex Hemphill (1957–95) is the gay poet and activist whose angry, explicit, autobiographical works went where few had gone before: he power-punched anti-gay attitudes, sexual objectification and racism, and helped define the experience of black gay men during the Aids epidemic.

Hemphill started to write in his teens; it was during a reading at Howard University, Washington, in 1980 that he first talked about being gay. His sensual, erotic poems and essays dealt with the anti-gay mindset of straight black men and the objectification of black men by the white gay community. No one was safe: Hemphill unpicked the work of celebrated queer photographer Robert Mapplethorpe, pointing out his images of black men were all dick, no face. And Jennie Livingston's legendary (and much loved) 1990 drag doc *Paris Is Burning*, according to Hemphill, revealed that the black drag performers' sassy imitations were 'materialistic, Caucasian and consumer' in nature.

In the late '80s, Hemphill brought energetic, visceral performances of his own work to small Washington DC venues, and – as his notoriety grew – to New York and London. His editing of anthology *Brother to Brother* (1991) won a Lambda literary award and his first full-length book, *Ceremonies* (1992), picked up the National Library Association's Gay, Lesbian, and Bisexual New Author Award.

Although something of a hidden hero, Hemphill has had an ever-lasting effect, inspiring other creatives from artists to performers – Justin Vivian Bond's (see page 48) dark, angry song *American Wedding* (2011) is powered by Hemphill's poetry, reimagined in a dark, angry drawl. Yet, as much as he inspired, he also provoked, and Hemphill's harsh takedown of race, sexuality, and masculinity is as uncomfortable and relevant as ever.

69

Candy Darling

Candy Says (1969) is Lou Reed's lullaby-soft tribute to glittering Warhol superstar Candy Darling, written at the height of her fame. The glamorous trans woman, actress, and scenester died five years later. She was just 29.

Born James Slattery, Darling (1944–74) spent her Long Island childhood obsessed with old Hollywood movies. She became skilled at mimicking the leading ladies that flickered on the screen and dreamed of being just like them. Darling enrolled at beauty school and began hanging out at the local gay hotspot. When her mother challenged her about rumours that her son was gay and a cross-dresser, Darling promptly went to her room, only to reappear in a dress. Or so the legend goes.

From then on, Darling dressed as she pleased. She'd travel into Manhattan, hanging out in Greenwich Village, making influential arty friends, changing her name numerous times until Candy Darling stuck. Warhol (see page 58) was fascinated with Darling and cast her in his film projects; she became a fixture at Warhol's Factory and soon found herself with something of a theatre and art-house movie career. Her short life was studded with celeb names and she became the muse of The Velvet Underground (as well as *Candy Says*, Darling is also name-checked in the Lou Reed's 1972 track *Walk on the Wild Side*).

Before she passed away after suffering lymphoma, she penned a letter to her friends. In it she said: 'I know I could've been a star but I decided I didn't want it.' But it seems that's just what she achieved. Call her what you will: a trans pioneer, a talented actress, the most glamourous member of the Factory; she was a true leading lady.

71

Oscar Wilde

'We are all in the gutter, but some of us are looking at the stars,' laments Lord Darlington in *Lady Windermere's Fan* (1892). Indeed, the play's author, Oscar Wilde (1854–1900) had his head craned up to the sky. In his lifetime (a tragically brief 46 years) the acerbic Irish novelist, essayist, playwright, and quip-machine published a catalogue of writing, from dark fairy tales and acidic comedies to classics like *The Picture of Dorian Gray* (1890) and *The Importance of Being Earnest* (1895).

Born into intellectual aristocracy, bouncy-haired Wilde balanced his career with international travel, lecture tours, and being the subject of the sizzling hot gossip that powered London society. In 1884, Wilde married Constance Lloyd and had two sons, but as he reached the pinnacle of personal confidence and success, he let go of the tight rein he kept on his sexuality. In 1886, he became friends (and perhaps lovers) with Canadian art critic and literary super-fan, Robbie Ross, who defied social convention and law and was openly gay. In 1891, Wilde began his infamously steamy affair with Lord Alfred Douglas, nicknamed 'Bosie', but four years later, along with Douglas, he felt emboldened enough to sue Bosie's influential father for libel after he publicly accused him of being gay.

Wilde lost everything. The case failed, details of his sex life were unveiled, and he was arrested for gross indecency and sentenced to two years' hard labour. On his release, he immediately moved to Paris, his health and reputation in tatters, and in his writing, his philosophy of happiness and humour decayed into darkness. Considering his social standing, literary achievements, glittering friendships and great loves, he found himself alone and destitute. Except for one – Robbie Ross – who was with him when he died.

Lily Tomlin

'When I recall my youth,' said Lily Tomlin (born 1939) on receiving the Screen Actors Guild Lifetime Achievement award in 2017, 'I can't point to a time when I showed promise to be anything but trouble.' The actor, singer and activist started out as a stand-up comic in Detroit and New York, landed a spot on *The Merv Griffith Show* (1965), developed her own iconic comedy characters – and has been trouble ever since.

In *Appearing Nitely* (1977), Tomlin became the first woman to appear solo in her own Broadway show. She also found roles in a slew of movie mega-hits, from Robert Altman's *Nashville* (1975) to *9 to 5* (1980) with Jane Fonda and Dolly Parton, but her later years have seen her experiment more with feminist and queer-edged projects.

The year *Nashville* made her a star, *Time* magazine offered to put her on the cover if she came out. Although Tomlin made no secret about her sexuality, it had never been reported. She had met her partner, the writer and producer Jane Wagner, in 1971 – it was love at first sight. The pair have worked and lived together ever since, and married in 2013. In the end, she declined *Time*'s offer, but has never shied away from being her true self. Known for her matter-of-fact, blunt way of speaking, bawdy stories, passionate activism, and volatility (there's a clip of her losing it on set of *I Heart Huckabees* in 2004 that is legendary), Lily Tomlin is the best kind of trouble.

Alan Turing

Genius computer scientist Alan Turing (1912–54) saved the world. From the invention of modern computing and artificial intelligence, to being instrumental to the Allies winning World War II, his legacy is overwhelming. Yet by the end of his life, this eccentric, creative, madcap man was hardly seen as a hero – in fact, quite the opposite.

Turing shone from the start. At 13, he was packed off to boarding school and, finding the strict way of teaching uninspiring, he studied on his own, becoming absorbed in Einstein's theory of relativity. At 17, he met with something altogether more complicated: Turing fell in love with his classmate, Christopher Morcom. But, when Christopher died suddenly, Turing was distraught.

At King's College, Cambridge, Turing's mathematical work was groundbreaking, and after two years at Princeton, he became a leading code-breaker at Bletchley Park, the UK code and cypher school. His work focused on cracking the Enigma cipher machine used by enemy forces and proved to be hugely important: his research and other inventions were integral to the war effort.

Turing's other works are considered the foundation of computer science; his Turing test advanced AI (via some tricky human versus machine chess matches), and his mathematical biology work informed later advances in DNA analysis.

Despite his patriotic work, OBE, and life-changing inventions, Turing was a victim of the era's anti-gay legislation. Convicted of gross indecency in 1952, he was dealt with harshly. He worried that news of his sexuality would cast a shadow over his scientific discoveries, and accepted hormone treatment rather than a prison sentence. In 1954, Turing was found dead at home – the coroner recording a verdict of suicide. He was a queer hero of science, human progress, and the pursuit of truth.

Michael Dillon

Gender warrior, doctor, writer, surgical pioneer, hero of the Blitz, and Buddhist monk, Michael Dillon (1915–62) lived many lives. He grew up with his brother and two aunts in Kent, England, graduated from Oxford (where he was president of the boat club) and took a job in a research lab. It would have been a rather calm existence had Michael ignored his true nature and not started the process of female to male transition.

Born Laura, Dillon had always lived as a woman, but as war broke out in Europe in 1939, he decided to start testosterone treatment. He worked in a garage, passed as male, and became a fire-watcher during the Blitz. He came to the attention of plastic surgeon Harold Gillies who, over the years, helped Dillon achieve a male body. In the meantime, Dillon studied medicine, changed his birth certificate, and worked hard to hide the paper trail that stated he was a woman.

Reading between the lines, bookish Dillon might have preferred a quieter existence, but his bravery in transforming his life, and others', meant he experienced something rather different. He helped Roberta Cowell become Britain's first trans woman to receive gender realignment surgery in 1951 and published a book about the experience. But in 1959, the press discovered Dillon had been born with a female body, and the resulting attention pushed Dillon to escape to India. There, he finally settled into a quiet life, studied Buddhist teachings, became ordained, and died in 1962.

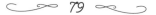

79

Madonna

The undefeatable power of pop and the tenacity of a woman who has spoken out for gay equality for decades make Madonna (born 1958) a queer hero.

In the 1980s, as Madonna first grappled with stardom (a pursuit, she has said, inspired by her gay ballet teacher, Christopher Flynn), she found herself deeply affected by the Aids crisis. Back then she was the punk-edged brat who hung out with the alt-art and dance crowd in NYC, and she lost many to the disease, including Keith Haring (see page 22) and her great friend Martin Burgoyne. It kick-started a lifetime of advocacy for people with Aids. Madonna performed at benefit gigs, made donations, and used her fame to push awareness and further understanding of gay people. Her 1991 documentary *Truth or Dare* (aka *In Bed with Madonna*) made stars of the gay dancers in her Blonde Ambition tour, and throughout her career, she continued to speak out on gay equality issues from adoption to bullying.

Madonna has soundtracked the lives of generations of queer-minded people who see themselves reflected in her sex-positive songs and videos. With a different look, sound, and persona for each era, Madonna has had many guises, from the Hollywood glamour style of *Vogue* (1990) and the creepy health goth of *Frozen* (1998) to the Vegas cowgirl of *Music* (2000) and tipsy gym instructor look of *Hung Up* (2005). But it's the rough-edged 1980s NYC Madonna that resounds the most, the one who first chose to champion the rights of queer people.

Rachel Maddow

Rachel Maddow (born 1973) is the ultimate lesbian pin-up, a polished political commentator, writer and Emmy award-winner who, against the odds, has made a name for herself in the dudes' club of TV news journalism. Maddow's quiet confidence and methodical approach have garnered her millions of viewers who love her habit of ignoring the personalities of politicians and – refreshingly – focusing on their actions instead. It's because of this that people really *listen* to Maddow. A classic liberal, she leaves furious right-wingers frothing at the mouth, but her meticulous, fact-focused investigations are hard to dispute. And it's all delivered in a delightfully witty, if not subtly ironic way.

A perennial outsider, Maddow has an uneasy relationship with celebrity. At high school in California she was a moody teen, and as a young adult, she was especially bookish, graduating Stanford and Oxford University as a Rhodes scholar (the first out gay student to receive the award), and hoping for a life in dusty academia and Aids activism. It was on a radio show in Massachusetts in 1999 that Maddow first tried her hand at broadcast journalism, and in 2008 she drifted into TV news, briefly filling in for a more seasoned broadcaster. She was a hit, and later that year, *The Rachel Maddow Show* first aired.

In many ways, Maddow is still an outsider. She's one of the few openly gay news journalists in the US ('I do think that if you're gay you have a responsibility to come out,' Maddow has said), and happily dresses 'like a 13-year-old boy'. But Maddow doesn't want you to focus on her, or her lesbian heart-throb status, but the transformative power of great journalism.

Larry Kramer

In 1980s New York, award-winning gay writer, playwright, and trouble-maker-in-waiting Larry Kramer (born 1935) witnessed the stirrings of something awful. His friends were getting sick and no one seemed to know why. At the time, Kramer had never been involved in activism. He was successful and rich; his life in New York and Fire Island was full of gourmet dinners and hot dudes in Speedos, and was, so far, untouched by tragedy. But after inviting a group of men to his apartment to discuss this new disease with a doctor, he found himself compelled to help. He helped co-found Gay Men's Health Crisis the following year.

From the start, the actions of GMHC didn't satisfy Kramer's furious anger at attitudes towards the growing Aids epidemic. It was an organisation which raised funds and helped with social care for gay men with HIV and Aids, but Kramer wanted to go further, targeting the NYC mayor for funds, threatening closeted gay bureaucrats who failed to help, and penning *1,112 and Counting...* (1983), a scathing article in a gay paper designed to scare men out of their apathy towards the disease.

It was too much for some. Kramer's subsequent ejection from GMHC is documented in his autobiographical and acclaimed play *The Normal Heart* (1985) – in which he made sure the main character was as obnoxious as possible. In 1987, Kramer's longing for a truly tough-ass politically-motivated group helped form Act Up, the Aids Coalition to Unleash Power. They targeted government organisations and megacorps with direct action to publicise the lack of funds and treatment for people with HIV and Aids – and inspired hundreds of chapters in the US and Europe. Today, Kramer's Act Up is still fighting the good fight, and GMHC is a world leader in HIV prevention.

Laverne Cox

'I'm a black transgender chick from Mobile, Alabama, I grew up poor and working class, and I'm on the cover of magazines,' says actor, performer, writer, producer and civil rights activist Laverne Cox (born 1972). At a time when gender is re-examined, trans stories are finally heard, and new social theories, bathroom laws, and pronouns abound, there have been few unifying voices. Cox, a natural orator (read: charmer), has sought to build bridges as much as she has crossed swords, often taking a deep breath when she could quite rightly snap.

We listen to Cox because she's *been there*. She was dreadfully bullied as a child and attempted suicide at 11, but made her way through using dance and performance. She moved to NYC in her late teens, and began her transition. Acting gave Cox a platform to finally speak out. In 2013, cult women's prison TV drama *Orange is the New Black* launched Cox into the mainstream, and ever since she's perfectly calibrated her celebrity with talk shows, awards ceremonies and lectures, alongside her hair-flicking, basque-wearing wild side.

Modern media indicates a growing acceptance of trans people; *Time* magazine called it a 'tipping point' when they put Cox on the cover in 2014 – but she's quick to point out this acceptance has limits. Those celebratory *you go, girl* outpourings are generally reserved for trans women who can easily pass as female; who are glossy, sexy and stylish, with dream hair – like Cox. But using her own visibility, Cox consistently draws our attention to the other: trans people who do not fit the mould, from incarcerated sex workers to teens battling bathroom bills. Passionate and engaging, Cox reminds us that not fitting in and struggling to be your authentic self is something we can all relate to.

 87

Divine

To understand Divine (1945–88), look no further than the man who unleashed her: cult filmmaker John Waters, known affectionately as the 'Pope of Trash'. As the director of low-budget gross-out flicks like *Pink Flamingos* (1972), Waters put Divine in front of the camera and allowed the wonderfully grotesque drag superstar to do her worst.

Divine, or rather Harris Glenn Milstead, spent most of his childhood in Lutherville, Maryland, then a crushingly humdrum and conservative American suburb. Plump and girlish, Glenn was bullied at school, finally finding friendship via his neighbour, amateur film-maker Waters. Together, they created Divine, a big bad girl from the wrong side of the tracks. All bravado and bosoms, the dangerous drag monster first appeared in Waters' 1966 film *Roman Candles* and then *Eat Your Makeup* (1968). Divine helped Glenn reveal a hidden, hawkish talent, hell-bent on notoriety.

Through more films and appearances, Waters and Divine's gnarly audience of counterculture freaks and geeks grew into a devoted following, and a star was born. Theatre followed, more cinematic work, trash pop music releases, health challenges, debt, and then Waters' *Hairspray* (1988), where Divine was convinced to drop her glamour look to play the tragi-comic character Edna Turnblad to huge acclaim. Through all this, Glenn wished for an acting career of his own, away from Divine, yet successful auditions rarely secured him a role. Finally, in 1988, he achieved his dream: a spot on the comedy show *Married... With Children*. Sadly, Glenn died of an enlarged heart the night before filming.

Although the infamous scene in *Pink Flamingos* where Divine eats dog poop seems to be Glenn's career-defining moment, perhaps we should first remember his jaw-dropping mastery of gender, taste, high camp and a brazen, busty queerness.

 89

Stephen Tennant

In the 1930s, to live and love openly as a gay man, to flirt outrageously with gender, excess, and a coterie of famous authors, and to flip a manicured finger at a shrill, conservative press would have required superhero strength. Luckily, spindly Brit Stephen Tennant (1906–87) had it in spades.

Tennant was a key player in the gossipy boho society satirised by Evelyn Waugh in *Vile Bodies* (1930), and in the late 1920s and early 1930s the papers frothed over the party boy and his gang's pre-war shenanigans powered by champagne, costume parties and what PG Wodehouse described as 'naughty salt'.

Described by sculptor Jacob Epstein as 'the most beautiful person, male or female, of his generation' and as a 'bird of paradise' by Virginia Woolf (see page 50), Tennant inspired any number of literary characters – not least Sebastian in Waugh's *Brideshead Revisited* (1945). He romanced Siegfried Sassoon, commanded audiences with Jean Genet and Greta Garbo, and developed a love of silk dressing gowns, leopard-print pyjamas and fluffy chinchilla collars. Tennant's noble lineage, class and wealth made him near untouchable to critique and his unique sense of style – a little lipstick here, a pair of earrings there – was wonderfully indulgent.

When he returned to his childhood home, Wilsford Manor, to spend the final 17 years of his life lounging regally in bed (apart from the odd visit to sleepy country villages dressed in pink micro-shorts or a tablecloth for a skirt), his devotees, including Christopher Isherwood (see page 12) and David Hockney, continued to visit.

Tennant's official legacy may be the artistic creations he inspired (he had little in the way of his own accomplishments), but it was the act of living life on your own terms – albeit as fantastically as possible – that he did so well.

91

Allen Ginsberg

Allen Ginsberg (1926–97) is the frizz-haired beat poet known for his deliciously filthy, potent writing that dealt in sweaty, man-on-man sex with a shocking frankness (his 1968 poem 'Please Master' is a real eyebrow-raiser).

As a young geeky teenager in New Jersey, Ginsberg would read Walt Whitman and write letters about political issues to *The New York Times*, but it was in 1943 at Columbia University, New York, that he met William Burroughs and Jack Kerouac. Drugs, drink, sex, handling stolen goods – and writing – followed. In 1954, he moved to San Francisco, and it's there, because of Ginsberg and his friends, that the Beat Movement flourished. Two years later, Ginsberg published 'Howl', his great gift to the world. The rambling poem is an outcry of rage at the state of post-war America, splicing pop culture with the literary avant-garde, and made Ginsberg famous (not least because it became the subject of an obscenity trial in 1957).

For Ginsberg, exploring the outer limits of human intellect, and living a radical, non-conformist life, was everything. Loving other men, and rising above sexual repression, was an essential part of this. And didn't he love to talk about it: he was deported from Cuba in 1965 for protesting about the government's persecution of gay people and describing Che Guevara as 'cute'.

Ginsberg met fellow poet Peter Orlovsky in 1954, and they stayed together in a loose, loving partnership for 43 years until Ginsberg's death in 1997. There was nothing private about Ginsberg, no secrets. Even in his later years, he would travel the world, give readings, and flirt with young men at after parties. His was a bawdy, passionate and eventful life lived large.

93

Ellen DeGeneres

Ellen DeGeneres (born 1958) is the mile-a-minute, high-energy comic, talk show host, actor, and business-leader whose infamous refusal of a puppy caused a seismic shift in attitudes towards queer people on TV – and pop culture at large.

Born in Louisiana, DeGeneres was waitressing and bartending when she started to perform comedy in cafes and clubs. Soon, she began touring her stand-up gig and was named Showtime's Funniest Person in America in 1982; a meandering career in TV finally lead to her scoring her own sitcom in 1994, inspired in part by her comedy routines. But in 1997, her primetime ABC show, *Ellen*, was in crisis. DeGeneres wanted her character to come out on air but, after months of negotiations with reluctant TV execs, it was suggested she get a puppy instead. DeGeneres had come out herself on *The Oprah Winfrey Show*, but for her sitcom character to do the same would have been a landmark (read: contentious) moment in TV history. She refused the puppy and, eventually, the network relented. The star-studded two-parter attracted 42 million viewers and led to advertiser boycotts, an Emmy, and the eventual cancellation of *Ellen*'s third season.

But what effect did DeGeneres' steadfastness ultimately have? At the time, she represented a painfully wholesome queerness – all tapestry waistcoats, cute sweaters, glossy bangs and neuroses – she was easy to love. But placing a gay main character on primetime TV, and into the homes of millions, had never been done, and helped to change attitudes towards LGBT+ people. More gay characters turned up on America's favourite shows, queer sitcom *Will & Grace* launched and became NBC's best-rated series, and today there are more gay people on TV than ever. As sweetly unthreatening as DeGeneres' queerness may have been, she arguably did as much for gay people as any politician or activist of the time. Just don't mention the puppy.

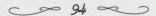

95

Marlene Dietrich

Much has been written about the odd morals of old Hollywood: how our favourite, butter-wouldn't-melt film stars lived altogether more unexpected, extraordinarily naughty lives off screen. According to historians, legendary German actor and singer Marlene Dietrich (1901–92) was no exception.

The star of *Dishonoured* (1931), *Shanghai Express* (1932), and *Blonde Venus* (1932) was a young upstart in the Berlin theatrical community before moving to the US. After World War I, a wonderfully decadent period of sexual exploration and creative freedom took hold in the uneasy Weimar Republic. It was there Dietrich's sexual confidence was unleashed; there are bawdy stories of backstage liaisons, sticky affairs, and the underwear of beautiful women ripped clean off (it was Dietrich who did the ripping). And it was during the filming of *The Joyless Street* (1925) that Dietrich and screen star Greta Garbo are said to have had a torrid affair, although the pair claimed not to know each other after their Hollywood reinvention.

There is something deliciously defiant about Dietrich. Unwavering self-belief saw her roll her eyes at conventional notions of gender and sex: she studied boxing, wore men's clothes, bedded the world's most beautiful women, and apparently slept with three Kennedys. In fact, Dietrich slept with anyone she wanted to. She once claimed: 'In Europe, it doesn't matter if you're a man or a woman – we make love to anyone we find attractive.'

Stories of Dietrich's antics – gossip, snobbery, competitiveness – seem to reveal a cruel character, but there was (even) more hidden behind the façade. In the late '30s, Dietrich and other high profile Germans set up a fund to help Jews and others escape the war, and in 1937 she donated her entire fee for *Knight Without Armour* to the refugees.

Armistead Maupin

Novelist Armistead Maupin (born 1944) is the queer Dickens, charting the highs and lows of San Francisco through the lives of a family of beloved characters who have (mostly) survived his ambitious nine-book, decade-spanning *Tales of the City* literary epic. The millions of readers who have lived, loved, and grown old alongside Mouse, Mona, Mary Ann, and Mrs Madrigal, have also found themselves submerged in stories of queer urban life, the Aids crisis (Maupin was one of the first fiction writers to address the illness), trans identity, sex and ageing, Quaaludes, and tighty-whitey dance contests.

Tales started as a serial in 1974 in a Marin County newspaper and Maupin soon found himself in a gruelling publishing schedule, churning out stories to deadline, weaving in contemporary issues and his own salty experience of the city. Like *Vertigo*, *Bullitt*, and other iconic San Francisco-set works, Maupin's *Tales* seemed less to reflect the reality of life in the city as much as add to its mythological status.

In 1974, when Mary Ann first discovered Barbary Lane, the fictional boarding house at the centre of the first novels, gay equality barely existed, at least outside of San Francisco. Slowly and steadily, works like *Tales* played a part in increasing the visibility of queer people. For Maupin, it has always been an intensely personal project; almost autobiographical. 'It was happening to me,' he explains, 'I was coming out to my own parents in the course of writing *Tales*.' He knew that, to change attitudes, 'all I had to do was to show how much fun it was to live my life, and to tell other people [not to] let that stigma weigh you down.'

99

Eleanor Roosevelt

In 1978, archivists at the Franklin D Roosevelt Library discovered 18 boxes of letters exchanged between First Lady Eleanor Roosevelt (1884–1962) and Lorena 'Hick' Hickok, the Associated Press reporter assigned to her. Over 30 years, the two women wrote almost 4,000 letters to each other, and their contents, much to the excitement of lesbians all over the world, implied something a little more than friendship.

To many, this came as something of a surprise, but to others, it seemed to fit what was already known about Eleanor's sapphic band of gal pals. For years, she lived with two gay women at her cottage in upstate New York, and in bohemian Greenwich Village, her closest friends were another lesbian couple whom she invited to political events, even to meet the British royal family.

Before, during and after her role as First Lady, Eleanor was politically active, a staunch advocate of civil rights – a hugely controversial stance at the time – and pushed for better roles for women in the workplace. When she was 15, Eleanor became a student at the Allenwood Academy in London with its gay feminist head teacher Marie Souvestre; it is thought to have been a major influence on her political outlook.

So, what of her relationship with Hick? The letters are steeped with longing and affection, talk of kissing and holding, and the frustration of being apart. Still, historians and biographers have different understandings of their meaning and, although Eleanor's openness and affinity with queer people was well known, the true nature of her relationship with Hick is a little unclear. On 9 April, 1934, Eleanor wrote Hick a one-line letter that seems to shine out: 'This is just a note to tell you I love you.'

Leigh Bowery

'Modern art on legs' is how Boy George once described Leigh Bowery (1961–94), the voluptuous fashion icon, performance artist and full-time outrage-machine. As fellow club creatures, George had a dancefloor's eye view of Bowery, and witnessed his evolution from nightlife personality to international art superstar.

Born in Sunshine, Australia, Bowery was lured to London by the burgeoning post-punk scene and set about constructing a new, polka-dotted, queer persona for himself. For each appearance, Bowery rebuilt his plump form with makeup, masks, and costume, adding wigs, dripping paint, or deformities, each look more outrageous than before. As a performer, just when it seemed he couldn't go any further, he would. From 'giving birth' on stage to performing an enema on himself, and then spraying down the audience, Bowery delighted and infuriated in equal measure.

Stories of the 1980s London creative scene always seem to have Bowery at the heart: his short-lived club night Taboo, a two-week stint at the Anthony d'Offay Gallery where he posed behind a two-way mirror, and becoming the muse of painter Lucien Freud who, it is said, was romanced by Bowery's legs. Defying convention at every turn, Bowery powered his art, design, and everyday existence with an unshakable sense of self. Bowery described himself as gay, but married his long-time friend Nicola Bateman in 1994, months before his death from an Aids-related illness on New Year's Eve.

His legacy lives on through the people he left behind, from Sue Tilley (his friend, champion, and also a model for Lucien Freud), to the designers, performers and artists who were lucky enough to bear witness to Bowery's technicolour greatness.

Ron Woodroof

Ron Woodroof (1950–92) is the ultimate drugstore cowboy. As the Dallas-born bisexual smooth-talker, Woodroof's dogged fight against bureaucracy, prejudice, and Aids made him a modern folk hero.

Woodroof was diagnosed with HIV in the mid-1980s. Prescribed AZT (a drug that nearly killed him) and given 30 days to live, he also lost his friends and, after his third divorce, faced the future alone. It was the height of Aids paranoia: the disease was spreading like wildfire, it was completely misunderstood, and the Federal Drug Agency's response to trialling new treatments seemed to move in slow motion. Meanwhile, thousands were dying, and Woodroof knew that he had to do something. He discovered successful antiviral treatments only available outside the US, cashed in his life insurance policy for capital and, by March 1988, his Dallas Buyers Club was formed.

Woodroof's apartment became a one-stop shop for experimental HIV and Aids treatments for American patients, and the club relied on a vast network of legal reps, judges, nationally recognised doctors, airline attendants, and friends at the border who all helped keep the project hidden from the FDA. Woodroof's Mexican drug runs required elaborate disguises to get back across the border (he did this more than 300 times); his incredible confidence in flouting the rules, and anger at the authorities is jaw-dropping. Woodroof died in 1992 of an Aids-related illness, six years after he was told he would die in days. In the end, his tenacity, risk-taking attitude and big Texan balls extended his own life, and potentially the lives of hundreds of others.

Frida Kahlo

For many years after her death, Frida Kahlo (1907–54) was kept in the shadows, known simply as the wife of Diego Rivera, the celebrated Mexican artist. Slowly, her posthumous fame eclipsed his, making her arguably the world's most famous female artist, and her sexuality and leftfield approach to gender, class and race finally revealed itself.

Kahlo dealt in revolution, pain and love. Her paintings – often self-portraits – underlined her own personal style. As a feminist pin-up and angry taboo-breaker, she styled herself in traditional Mexican clothing with flowers and scarves in her hair, making a nationalist political statement (perhaps somewhat lost on the kids who dress as her at modern-day costume parties).

Born in Mexico City, Kahlo contracted polio as a child, and survived a bus crash in her teens that left her with bouts of intense pain and difficult surgeries for the rest of her life. Kahlo had an infamously volatile marriage with Rivera, but also navigated relationships with a number of women, including Josephine Baker. But her queer hero status is based on more than just flings with women; it comes from Kahlo's incredible female sexual confidence, often dragging up (rather handsomely) in men's clothing. Her angry rejection of normative behaviour was completely at odds with 1930s, '40s, and '50s macho society.

More Queer Heroes Who Changed the World

Award-winning choreographer and sassy modern-dance supremo, *Alvin Ailey*

The godfather of civil rights, *Bayard Rustin*, advocated for gay equality in the '80s

Former No. 1 tennis champ, *Billie Jean King*, was the first professional female athlete to come out as lesbian

Writer, painter and out gay man during the Harlem Renaissance, *Richard Bruce Nugent*

Aboriginal Australian rugby player *Casey Conway* who speaks out at the lack of acceptance of gay people

Impossibly cool lesbian Belgian film maker *Chantal Akerman* who focused on female desire

Pastel-haired pop icon, Aids activist and LGBT+ homeless teen supporter, *Cyndi Lauper*

David Bowie, the skinny ginger polymath whose non-conformist stance continues to inspire the queer-minded

Incorrigibly cheeky artist and bespectacled British national treasure, *David Hockney*

NYC painter, photographer, writer, filmmaker, performance artist, and Aids activist, *David Wojnarovicz*

Cult film maker *Gregg Araki*, director of *Mysterious Skin*, and major player in the '90s New Queer Cinema movement

Indie film maker and music video creative *Gus Van Sant*, director of *Drugstore Cowboy*, *Milk*, and *My Own Private Idaho*

Broodingly handsome screen icon, *James Dean*

American lesbian entertainer, activist and French secret agent, *Josephine Baker*

Gender theorist, trans activist, and 'Stay Alive' advocate, *Kate Bornstein*

Trailblazing African American 'mother of the blues', lesbian, *Ma Rainey*

The greatest female tennis player ever, *Martina Navratilova* is an outspoken advocate for gay equality

Art photographer and creator of iconic queer imagery, *Robert Mapplethorpe*

African American sci-fi writer, literary critic and beardy professor, *Samuel Delany*

Celebrated novelist and master of the historical lesbian romp, *Sarah Waters*

South African *Simon Nkoli*, the anti-apartheid, gay equality and civil rights activist

Pioneer of New Queer Cinema, American indie film maker and producer, *Todd Haynes*

Dancer, choreographor, vogueing champ, and star of *Paris is Burning, Willi Ninja*

About the Author

Dan Jones is a writer based in London. A former shopping editor at *i-D* magazine and style editor at *Time Out* magazine, he is also the author of *The Mixer's Manual*, *Man Made*, *Gin*, and *Rum*.

Acknowledgements

Thanks to illustrator Michele Rosenthal (whose amazing *Queer Portraits in History* project inspired this book), queer consultant Kate Jinx, superstar designer Nicky Barneby, plus Hannah Roberts, Kate Pollard, and all the heroes at Hardie Grant.

50 Queers Who Changed the World

by Dan Jones

First published in 2017 by Hardie Grant Books, an imprint of Hardie Grant Publishing

Hardie Grant Books (UK)
52–54 Southwark Street
London SE1 1UN

Hardie Grant Books (Australia)
Ground Floor
Building 1
658 Church Street
Melbourne, VIC 3121

hardiegrantbooks.com

The moral rights of Dan Jones to be identified as the author
of this work have been asserted by him in accordance with the
Copyright, Designs and Patents Act 1988.

Text © Dan Jones 2017
Illustrations © Michele Rosenthal 2017

All rights reserved. No part of this publication may be
reproduced, stored in a retrieval system or transmitted in any form by
any means, electronic, electrostatic, magnetic tape, mechanical,
photocopying, recording or otherwise, without the
prior written permission of the Publisher.

British Library Cataloguing-in-Publication Data. A catalogue record
for this book is available from the British Library.

ISBN: 978-1-78488-134-4

Publisher: Kate Pollard
Senior Editor: Kajal Mistry
Commissioning Editor: Hannah Roberts
Publishing Assistant: Eila Purvis
Illustrator: Michele Rosenthal
Art Direction: Nicky Barneby
Production Controller: Jess Otway
Colour Reproduction by p2d

Printed and bound in China by Leo Printing Group